THIS HAVE I DONE FOR YOU

.....What have you done for me (JESUS)..

By

EVANGELIST MICHAEL C. OLUA

DEDICATION

I dedicate this book to my Lord and Saviour JESUS Christ and God The Father: who really desire all men to be saved and come to His fullness and perfect Will.

CONTENTS

	Title Page		i
	Copyright		
	Dedication		
	THIS HAVE I DONE FOR YOU		
1	Chapter One	JESUS Throne	1 – 10
2	Chapter Two	Sorrowful Heart	11 – 15
3	Chapter Three	Condemned to Death	16 – 22
4	Chapter Four	Calvary	23 - 27

CHAPTER ONE

JESUS Throne

Have you ever wondered, or asked yourself this question "Why did or what made Jesus leave his glorious Throne and Crown to come down here on earth and died for you?" Many have not thought of that, neither have they sit to think about it because they are too busy doing one thing or the other to satisfy their own self and they do only what will satisfy their flesh, and what they will glory on only, forgetting the main thing they have to do and also satisfy! Now let's imagine how this Glorious Throne that Jesus left just for your sake is! This Glory cannot be qualified with anything here on earth because in his kingdom are found many precious things even the things that came into existence came from above, from the Most Excellency. Jesus has been in existence before the foundation of this world and He has been with the Father, the God Almighty, the source of all powers, authority and Dominion, and by His great power through His Son Jesus Christ created he everything that are in existence both the visible and the invisible Col. 1:16. Jesus knowing how excellent, pure, worthy and unfailing the glory and Majesty of His Father was, is and will always be, he prayed in John 17:5 "And now, O Father, glorify thou me with thine own self with the glory which I had with thee before the world was". Jesus knowing, also how mighty His Father is, humbles himself always before Him and seeking how to please the Father the more and how to Bless his Holy name, he found no other way but to be totally humble and doing His Fathers, will always. Because of this, God loved and loves him so much that he (God) honours him (JESUS - The Word) more than any other things. Before the foundation of the world, creation of angels, even heaven, Jesus has been, and through him did everything exist, I mean everything even Satan, Lucifer that old serpent was created through Jesus and for Jesus. "For by him were all things created, that are in heaven, and that are in earth, visible and invisible, whether they be thrones, or dominions, or principalities, or powers: all things were created by him, and for him:" Col. 1:16. Because all things were created through him and for him, they are subject to him (Jesus) and they are been put under him (Jesus) so that the Father will be glorified in him and through him. Therefore because of this, whatever or whosoever he loves, he makes it more humble, and perfected both in beauty, in knowledge and in wisdom and then lift such up to be like him (Jesus). Whatsoever Jesus loves, is loved by God and whatsoever Jesus hates has already be hated by God, likewise, whosoever and whatsoever is loved by God Jesus loves, whatsoever is hated by God Jesus hates because he and his Father are one. Lucifer was privileged to be loved by God through Jesus, and because of this was he (Lucifer) made perfect in beauty, knowledge, he had the wisdom of God, also was he made the light of God, because of his closeness with God and communication made him think that he is the mouth by which God speaks. The words from Lucifer's mouth was perfect and always executed, with this, he (Lucifer) thought that God has no say any more and that his (Lucifer) wisdom and words are now more powerful than God's own not knowing that the wisdom he had was "JESUS' and also the words which he (Lucifer) speak and was perfect, was "JESUS" also the power he had was "Christ" 1 Cor. 1:24, everything Lucifer thought he had was Jesus, even the bright morning star Lucifer was made was also Jesus and the bible made it clear in I Corinthians 1:24 "but for those whom God has called, both Jews and Gentiles, this message is Christ, who is the power of God...." also in I Corinthians 1:30 "But God has bought you into union with Christ Jesus, and God has made

Christ to be our Wisdom…" Jesus, also in Revelation 22:16 say that "… I am the root and the offspring of David, and the bright and morning star". There was nothing of greatness Lucifer will think of that was not given to him by God through Jesus. And to tell you that the perfect wisdom is found in Christ Jesus by God even before the creation of anything, the day Lucifer thought of pride did Jesus (Pure Wisdom) left him (Lucifer). When Jesus left him, he never knew and he (Lucifer) now depended on his own understanding and wisdom that made him believe that he (Lucifer) is greater than God and need to build or even sit above the Throne of God Almighty. As the Spirit of God left Saul, so did the Spirit of God left the son of down/morning(Lucifer) it was after the Spirit Left Lucifer that the name "MICHAEL" in heavenly Language, meaning " Who is Like God" was highly established in heaven, to make it known to every powers, principalities, domination and authorities in heaven and of heaven ,that God is the "JEHOVAH" meaning "SELF EXISTING ONE" and "EL SHADAI" meaning "ALMIGHTY GOD" After making this known, Satan still went more further to deceive as many angels he can which with the deceived angels, broke out war in heaven. The angels of God fought Lucifer and his angels proclaiming "There is none Like unto God" Michael whom God has already prepared for such a battle, prevailed with many other angels of God with him .After this God never again gave perfection to any again accept Jesus (The Word of God) who was so much submissive and humble to God, because of this did God lift his name (Jesus) high above every other name that at the mention of that name Jesus, every kneel must bow and tongue confess that Jesus is Lord. Philippians 2:8-11.God now resist the proud and give grace to the humble through Jesus. In the kingdom of God, Jesus is also a king, even the KING of Kings and the LORD of Lords of whom is the beauty of the angels, He is the smile of the angels, hope of the saints and resurrection into glory. All this Glory, even the worship of his angels left he in the kingdom of his Father to take the filthy body of man, He Left His Glorious Spiritual being to dwell in the dusty body, He left his Glorious riches of heaven and made himself poor all for our sake, He left his Glorious resting throne and came down to walk and work for your sake, that all may be well with you! What a great Shepherd he is for a hireling does not care about the sheep he looks after but the shepherd that owns the sheep will not only look after or take care of the sheep but he will also lay down his life for his sheep because he so much Love them. Truly I tell you no man can do what Jesus has done, His humbleness, is more than too much, His Love unspeakable, what else will I say if not, "THANK You JESUS" for all things. If then that he counted all as lost and then left all aside to come down to save you , You are expected to count all as lost, so as to gain the Excellency of the knowledge of Christ (Phil 3:8), and make him happy always. It's a challenge to all living being. Do not say "it is not easy", for Jesus had the same body you have today, was tried and tempted but He never failed, for He (JESUS) ever trusted and looked upon the Father's grace and help. The same way are we to hope and look unto Jesus the author and finisher of our faith for victory over all things (Heb 12:2). Amen.

CHAPTER TWO

Sorrowful Heart

After God asked "Who shall go for us" no one accepted to go, seeing all punishment that follows, all the agony, all the passion that must be fulfilled before our (humanity) soul will be redeemed, seeing this, all (in heaven) kept silent, and to fulfill the prophecy which says "He bore our sins and carried our infirmity and by his strips we are healed". It was in him alone was found worthy to bear all these, because of his love for us all. As the Father loves us, so do he love us also that made him to bring himself so low. By the grace of God a woman was favoured by God to be used as an instrument and a vessel of which the Saviour was born to suffer for mankind. I have never seen a man who is like Jesus, the bible says He grew up with the fear of God and did what was right both in the sight of man and of God. From the day Jesus started his ministry here on earth, a great burden was ahead waiting for him, though when he started, his mind was to bring together the disciples who he shall sanctify and make clean by the word of God. It took Jesus his sleep to work toward seeing that both his disciples and we are made clean by his word and also saved in him, and the only way to save them is to make his Father known unto them both by words and works. Day and night did Jesus strive to see that all things which have been written and prophesied about him may come to pass unto the glory of his Father in heaven. He saw no reason to be discouraged since he is working toward our victory and freedom that we may no longer live in bondage. When the hour drew near, he remembered once again the cup that his Father have given that he must drink, when he remembers this, his heart sorrows. Even at the last supper said he in Luke 22:14-15 "And when the hour was come, he sat down, and the twelve apostles with him. v15: And he said unto them, with desire I have desired to eat this Passover with you before I suffer". This he knew that he must suffer for the sake of human that they may be redeemed. The bible said that, even when he went to pray, his heart was sorrowful that he wished that his own will would be done, but being obedient and wanting the will of his Father alone to be done, he prayed that the Father's will may be done. No man can bear such which Jesus went through when he went to pray, he took Peter and the two sons of Zebedee. The bible said he became sorrowful and very heavy (KJV), and Good News Bible would say "grief and anguish came over him". He was so much disturbed and grieved that he has to speak out to his disciple saying "The sorrow in my heart is so great that it almost crushed me" (Mathew 26:38 GN). Now I ask you the reader have your heart ever been troubled and so much disturbed? Have you ever been in a situation that you find your heart being crushed inside? By worry? Or thinking? Or let me say, both? If you can feel such a way in a little situation, yea, I call it a little situation and condition because it can never, and never can be compared with the condition and situation Jesus was at Gethsemane where he cried out bitterly and his sweat was like drops of blood to show the kind of grief he was into, both his body, soul, spirit and mind was grieved all for you: fornicators, liars, immoral, thieves, murderers, supporters of evil, all these he did was for us sinners. He left his disciples aside and went a little farther on, and threw himself face downwards on the ground, and prayed "My father, if it is possible, take this cup of suffering from me! Here Jesus has to approach the Almighty as in the form of "Father and son". Already Jesus knows how painful it will be as was shared and commanded unto him by his Father, in heaven. But Jesus at this junction remembered something (I speak as a man), he remembered how you that is in sorrow now will be joyful, he remembered how you a sinner will be turned away from sin, he remembered how you that is in difficulties will be comforted, he remembered how special you are to him and how much he loves you, which quotes "Greater love has no man than to lay down his life for his friends" and because he is subjected and bound to be humble and to the will of God (Hebrews 10:5-7, it say "v5: for this reason, when Christ was also out to come into the world, he said to God: 'You do not want sacrifices and offerings, but you have prepared a body for me. v6: You are not pleased with animals burnt whole on the altar or with sacrifices to take away sins. v7: Then I (Jesus) said, 'here I am to do your will, O God just as it is written of me in the book of the law'. (GN). Though in all this grief, he was submissive to God that he concluded his prayer of Mathew 26:39 by saying. "….Nevertheless not as I will, but as thou wilt. This same prayer he prayed again after meeting and found his three disciples sleeping, he went back again and prayed to his Father. The bible said in Luke 22:42-44, that, he prayed to the extent the angel of God came and strengthened him. Jesus prayed, even his sweat was like drops of blood falling to the ground. If God can give his Son and leave him to fulfill his will here on earth all because of you, what else do you want God to do for you before you realize that He loves you, what else will he do before you acknowledge him as your personal Lord and Saviour.

* * * * * *

Lord Jesus I know that you never refused to pass all these things for my sake all because of your love for me and to save my soul. I know how I do feel when my heart is troubled, even when am found at fault, how much more you who was innocent in all the false words spoken to condemn you for my sake, I want to say thank you for accepting the sorrow with all your heart. I pray I do more for thee.

* * * * * *

After his prayer to God the Father he had to take that bitter pill, even I will say, that he had to swallow the bitter pill of Gods will which was very difficult. He after being strengthened by the angel of God, he had to take his stand and went to his disciples and said "Arise for the hour has come that the son of man must be handed over" As it was written that he shall be betrayed by the same person that ate with him. One of the most painful part of it was that his disciple left him alone in the hands of his enemy, who slapped him pinched him and asked him to tell them who did that to him. These people had no fear in them; they treated him like a thief all for our sake. Even when he needed the comfort of his Father, his Father turned his back on him because the sins of the whole world was upon him (God did this because he the Lord God is too Holy to behold iniquity) Habb 1:13. How will you feel when you are captured and your father is there, you can see him and you cry unto him for help, and he turn his back on you and the only thing he can do is to cry even when you know he has the power to save you but he did not because of the people that don't love him? Some will say that such father is very wicked if he does that. But imagine how much it was with Jesus whom has been crushed in heart, left by his disciples, coming again to be left by his own Father! All this was because of you, both you the reader and the whole world, now if God have risked his Son Jesus Christ to save us, and also Jesus risking his throne and Glory in heaven to come down to suffer for you, what have you then done for him? Jesus is speaking to us all both the unrighteous and the righteous ones, the believer and the unbelievers, even more especially to us ward and his children, whom he have bought by his blood, what have you done for him? You claim to be a Pastor? How many souls have you really brought to Jesus? You have forgotten his death and have given your mind to money, because of your title as a Bishop, Most Rev. etc. Marching upon the souls you are to bring to JESUS. You are now too big to go out for evangelism. Don't you know that, no matter the post/position a demon has in hell, they still go out to win and get more souls that do not belong to them? You that say that Jesus has abandoned you, if Jesus did not give up when he was suffering for you on earth, is it now he is sitting Gloriously at the right of the Father that he will forget you? Arise and go forth and do something for the Lord God because your situations are settled before him. There is no body that feels and knows your condition except he who sorrowed and shed his blood for you, and for this reason, your broken heart is healed. Pray Him to come to your soul, pray him to release the precious flow of the blood which can wash you and make you whole again. How many of you are ever ready to do more than he hath done for you, how many of you have sleepless night because of the work of the Father? But blessed are they who die daily in Christ for their works are not in vain. 1 Cor 15:58.

CHAPTER THREE

Condemned To Death

Throughout the night, he was awake in pains, being blamed, bearing all alone, and no water passed through, nor touched his lips, to quench his thirst, he only substituted his saliva as drinking water. He was tempted and trailed; he was and is the word that became flesh which bore my sin and death. He was innocent but yet counted as a sinner just to make sure we are made the righteousness of God in Him, they killed Him, but killing him made all things new and marked the beginning of a new dawn. Though there was nothing to hold hand that he did but still the priests and the people he loved and came to die for rejected him. Like a sheep, he did not talk nor say anything, but all he care for was to beheld the cross with which the sins of man was wiped away, and priests forgiven, what a merciful friend, what a merciful Father, what a merciful one, more than a friend to me and to us all. The mediator, by whom and for whom all things were created both visible and invisible, the only begotten of the Father (JEHOVAH). Jesus cherished the old rugged cross, with the pains in his body, he held unto the cross firmly with tears in his eyes, he kept on walking towards Calvary, he was never discouraged nor ashamed to bear the sins of all, though he was not guilty, he prepared to bear guilt of all, so that through this, we may be blameless before the Father. The bible said "The high priest questioned Jesus about his disciples and about his teaching. Jesus answered "I have always spoken publicly to everyone, all my teaching was done in the synagogues and in the temple, where all the people come together. I have never said anything in secret. Why, then do you question me? Question the people who heard me. Ask them what I told them-they know what I said. When Jesus said this, one of the guards there slapped him and said," How dare you talk like that to the High Priest". Jesus answered him, "if I have said anything wrong, tell everyone here, what it was. But if I am right in what I have said, why do you hit me?" Early in the morning Jesus was taking from Caiaphas' house to the governor's palace. The Jewish authorities did not go inside the palace, for they wanted to keep themselves ritually clean, in order to be able to eat the Passover meal. So Pilate went outside and asked," What do you accurse this man of? Their answer was. "We would not have brought him to you if he had not committed a crime." Pilate said to them, "Then you yourselves take him and try him according to your own law." They replied, "We are not allowed to put anyone to death." (This happened in order to make the words of Jesus come true, the words he used when he indicated the kind of death he would die.) Pilate went back into the palace and called Jesus "Are you the king of the Jews?" he asked him. Jesus answered, "Does this question come from you or have others told you about me? " Pilate replied, do you think I am a Jew? It was your own people and the chief priests who handed you over to me. What have you done?" Jesus said, "My kingdom does not belong to the world, if my kingdom belonged to the world, my followers would fight to keep me from being handed over to the Jewish authorities. No, my kingdom does not belong here" So Pilate asked him, "Are you a king, then? "Jesus answered, "You say that I am a king. I was born and came into the world for this one purpose, to speak about the truth. Whoever belongs to the truth listens to me. "And what is truth?" Pilate asked. Then Pilate went back outside to the people and said to them, "I cannot find any reason to condemn him. But according to the custom you have, I always set free a prisoner for you during the Passover. Do you want me to set free for you the king of the Jews?" They answered him with a shout, "No, not him! We want Barabbas!"

(Barabbas was a bandit). John 18:19-40. Pilate took Jesus and had him whipped. He was even mocked by solider as they put a crown made out of thorny branches on his head. Not minding the stripes on him, they all whom he (Jesus) healed their diseases and forgave their sin, it was the same people that welcomed him as a king, they all wished him death, even proclaimed it unto Pilate saying "Crucify him, Crucify him". You that is reading, may say or will say that this people are extremely wicked and heartless, not knowing that you have even done more than they have done, because once did they crucified him but you, most times crucify Jesus in your actions, words, deeds, ways and doings. We say that we love Jesus but our actions shows and say that we hate him. Hardly will you see a man or a woman who says that they are not Christians in our world today, all they say is that they are Christians, even the people that call themselves or will I say, who are meant to be the righteousness of God and a light to the world, they are now mixed up with the children of this world (children of disobedient), pursuing after shadows, pursuing after things that vanishes away and leaving the everlasting one, which is Jesus Christ. The bible said that it was because of the joy ahead of him (Jesus), endured all things to the end and because of this God exalted him and set his name above all names that at the mention of the name Jesus, every knee must bow and every tongue confess that Jesus is the King of Glory and the Lord of all. The most foolish thing this people have ever done is to crucify the king of Glory, they lack the wisdom mystery in his death, that why the bible said in 1 Corinthians 2:8 "…none of the princes of this world knew, for had they known it, they would not have crucified the Lord of Glory". But he accepted to go into this from the beginning of it all (in heaven) before he came down on earth. Jesus hungered and longed to die to deliver you and I, this also was why he looked toward Judas Iscariot of whom Satan entered and said "That which you would do, do it fast" John 13:27. This he said, was not because the suffering and persecution which he was about to face was sweet, but he said this because there is left no time to waste in order to deliver us all who were sinners, we who never loved him nor know him. Again at Gethsemane when they came to arrest him, and ask "Where is Jesus?" He did not deny accepting to give himself, twice they asked and he answered "I am He". The name "Jesus" means "Saviour" so therefore they asked "Where and who is the saviour?" Jesus said "I am He" meaning "I am He that will save both you (the officers and the whole world". If Jesus never loved us, he would have not accepted to die for us even, he would have prayed his Father in heaven and He would have send and give to him (Jesus) more than twelve legions of angels. (Mathew 26:53) to fight for him against the officers and the high priests, but he did not do that! For the joy ahead of him, he endured, knowing that he will be exalted so that by him we may be set free from the bondage of the enemy, also, he endured so as to claim for us, from the Father; Power and authority, grace and mercy to overcome temptations and sin, even Satan the father of all evil. They all said shouting "let his blood be upon us, even upon our children". They ignorantly don't know the meaning of what they all agreed on because if the blood of Jesus (who was innocent) was just an ordinary man's blood like that of Abel, it would have cried bitterly to God for vengeance and the Righteous God would have avenged it upon them and their children, even upon all their generation, but the blood of Jesus was not so, his blood worketh to the purifying of the soul, spirit, conscience and body for our everlasting redemption. The bible said in Hebrew 12:24, using Amplified version and it says "And to Jesus, the Mediator (Go- between, Agent) of a new Covenant, and to the sprinkled blood which speaks (of mercy), a better and noble and more gracious message than the blood of Abel (which cried out for vengeance)," so therefore if the blood of Jesus was like that of Abel's blood, being the Son of God, God would have even at that moment they said that, destroy them all, but the blood of Jesus is the blood full of love and ever ready to Sanctify, purify and make one whole. Because of the working of the blood of Jesus to the saving of our soul and remission of sin, it therefore went upon their head and of their children not to destroy them, but to save them and wash their sins away and put them right with God, "to wit, that God was in Christ, reconciling the world to Himself, not imputing their trespasses unto them..." 2 Cor 5:19. This blood flowed even down to us, that we may obtain mercy from God and not be utterly destroyed and condemned. The blood of Jesus became life to them which are dead, strength to them which are weak, and washes clean them which are dirty, and then, expecting them all to do, walk and work with the grace in that blood in order to please the Father and get themselves an everlasting inheritance in heaven. Humanity have misused the grace and making fresh the memory to God the Father, the beatings and agony of his Son Jesus Christ. It would have been better to bring to memory to God the Father the beatings and agony Jesus went through in our plea for mercy and forgiveness of sin than to re-crucify the Son of God again through sin, evil and wicked deeds. He who wants to follow the Lord Jesus must deny himself and carry his cross and follow him, knowing that all that will live godly in Christ Jesus shall suffer, in fact must suffer persecution. 2 Tim 3:12. The Lord Jesus through his mercy and grace granted me the opportunity and took my spirit in the dream, and in that dream, I was a dead man in my dream, and my spirit left and went up to a place where there was much persecution and agony as Christ went through, and many people were there, but as i was getting closer, they were leaving and could not endure the pains. So when I got close, only one young man was still there (determined to face it all). The young man I saw was already ahead of me in the persecution and suffering called "crucifixion procedure", I wanted to quit and go back to the world, but they said that there was no going back, so I had to go ahead to suffer the beatings and strips, that was almost exactly the way Jesus suffered. (You may ask, have I seen or was I there when Jesus passed through all he went through?) But of a truth, I was totally whipped as by a Roman soldier and after which I thought it was over, the young man which I saw at the beginning now said to me "There is one side of your soul that you need to go to and stay for a while and after that you will be crucified on the cross" I was still wondering in that place saying "Those it mean that am dead for real? And after all these, if one is not qualified for heaven that means hell forever? God have mercy and help me". So as I was about to go to that side of my soul to stay as was told me by the young man, I saw how they nail him on the cross and he was crying, so when I saw that the young man had the heart to accept that such, I then said to them, please crucify me too so that I can be partaker of Christ suffering". By the grace and peace of God that passeth all understanding, I was given the interpretation of that dream; As soon as you are born again, you are dead to the world and alive unto righteousness and anyone who must not go back to the world but continue with God in Christ must partake in the sufferings of Christ JESUS our Lord, but they that cannot hold on will abandon their faith, just as I saw from afar many, but getting close, so many left but only one stayed and held on. In Acts 14:22, it says "...we must through much tribulation enter into the kingdom of God. Of a truth I tell you brethren, any Christianity that offers you the whole world even heaven, without the suffering in Christ Jesus, is not a genuine, neither is it a real Christian life. In Romans 8:36-37 it says "As it is written, for thy sake we are killed all the day long: we are accounted as sheep for the slaughter. Nay, in all these things we are more than conquerors through him that loved us" also in 2 Timothy 3:12.The bible says "You and all that will live godly in Christ Jesus shall suffer persecution". Therefore pray always that God makes you partakers of the sufferings of Christ Jesus, giving no offence in anything, that the ministry be not blamed: But in all things approving ourselves as the ministers of God, in much patience in afflictions, in necessities, in distress, in strips, in imprisonments, in tumults, in labours, in watchings, in fasting, By pureness, by knowledge, by longsuffering, by kindness, by the Holy Ghost, by love unfeigned (2 Cor 6:3-6), and I say, looking steadfast unto Jesus the author and finisher of all things whom he himself hath suffered being tempted, and is able to come quick to help those who are tempted also (Heb 2:18). Therefore as he for the sake of the joy ahead, looked upon the Father and was transformed from one glory to another glory and he is not just like God but he (Jesus) is also God Himself, let's look also steadfast unto Jesus without covering our face or taking your face off from Him that we may be transformed from one glory to another glory until we become not just like him, but as he is pure we shall be pure. 1 John 3:3. Amen.

CHAPTER FOUR

Calvary

All things was finished over there (Calvary) and for this reason, The Spirit put to remembrance unto the saints, the cross with which the sins of man was wiped away, with which man became whole again, with which man was reconnected to the Father. That same cross serves as the Lords closest best friend, for he held firmly unto it in pains and not minding, he looked steadfast unto the joy that was set before him and also having in mind to redeem his people by his own precious blood, such people are no other person but you and I and the whole world. Calvary has been a place for the crucifixion and execution of law breakers and normally called "sinners" who do not want to obey the command of the law, more especially the law (rules and regulations) of the Romans Empire. Calvary in Hebrew tongue is called "Golgotha" meaning a place of skulls. The place has been a place of sorrow, a painful sorrowful place for both the victim and relative who watch them die. Non ever wish to remember such a place, not until Jesus came and turned Calvary a into place of re-strengthening of faith, a place where sin is beheaded instead of human head which decay to be skulls, a place where our mortal bodies in faith is crucified with him (Christ Jesus) that we may now live a new life also in faith of him who died for us. In the time past, in the days of Abraham, even Elijah, the days when the temple has not yet been built, alters which were used for sacrifice unto God was built with stones and just for some while. They offered sacrifice which was acceptable unto God on stones. And when the building of the Temple which is in

Jerusalem was built, the body of the animals was burnt outside while their blood was taken inside by the priest into the Holy of Holies of the tabernacle. But Jesus made all things total different and new, being a high priest of good things to come, by a greater and more perfect tabernacle not made with hands, that is to say, not of this building, neither by the blood of goats and calves, but by his own blood he entered in once into the holy place (Heaven itself), having obtained eternal redemption for us. Heb 13:11-12. The blood that was shed for you and I works not only to the purifying of the flesh as the blood of bulls and of goats, and the ashes worked in the old but the blood of Jesus purified both the conscience and the flesh (inside and outside), it went both vertical and horizontally, it went Omni-directional, to wash, clean, purify, sanctify, and even stand as the perfect covenant and mediator of our sin and wrong in order to present us Holy and perfect without any spot, wrinkle or blame in/on us all. Amen. I strongly believe that the blood of Jesus is so much costly than we can think or even imagine. We all know that to buy a goat or bull is costly, which the poor can hardly afford and the rich can afford it, but even at that, if we were to be paying for our sin with the blood of goats, bulls and ash all the time both the poor and some rich cannot pay such, mostly, the poor ones who finds it difficult to feed and shelter for themselves and family. Flesh and blood cannot please God and man's righteousness is a fifthly rag unto God and also living in this wicked and sinful world, you can never defect sin out of your own power but only through Jesus. And even if you can afford to buy goats, you cannot afford "a blood" because it's the Lord that giveth blood and the blood in any living, is its life. Lev 17:11. Blood can speak and God heareth them because he gave it voice to cry out against any who splits it out unnecessary, He also gave it voice to speak, on behalf of another. And He (God) said to Cain, what hast thou done? The voice of thy brother's blood crieth unto me from the ground. Gen 4:10. The blood of Abel cried unto God for vengeance against his brother who had slain him, and God being a Righteous Judge, Judged Cain and gave to him his punishment in mercy. Also in Rev6:9-10, the bible says that the souls of the saints which were slain for the word of God and for the testimony which they held, they cried with a loud voice unto God saying, How long, O Lord, holy and true dost thou not judge and avenge our blood on them that dwell on the earth? God later in Rev 16:6 avenged their blood upon them that dwell on the earth! Rev 16:3-7 the bible says "And the second angle poured out his vial upon the sea, and it became as the blood of a dead man: and every living soul died in the sea v4; and the third angle poured of his vial upon the rivers and fountains of the waters; and they became blood v5; and I heard the angle of the waters say, thou art righteous, O Lord, which art and wast, and shalt be because thou hast judged thus.v6: for they have shed the blood of saints and prophets, and thou hast given them blood to drink; for they are worthy". If the blood of an animal can speak and work to purifying of the flesh just once a while, and blood of the innocents can cry continually till it avenged, then it stops crying, how much more the blood of him that knew not, know not and will never know sin, how much more his blood? His blood surpasses that of the animal by purifying not only the flesh but also the consciences, his blood also speaketh better thing more than the blood of Abel and the voice of his blood has no end for it continueth to speak both in this world and the world to come, his blood is the ink with which our names are written in the book of the Lamb(The book of Life), His blood speaks for the living who lives in him, and also for them which are asleep, who slept in him, so therefore whether we live or die we belong to Christ Jesus for we are redeemed by his blood. Amen. For this, therefore anyone whose name is not found written in the book of the Lamb of God, has rejected and trodden under foot his blood and they who have done that shall be crushed and destroyed by the same blood because the blood shall be against them. And all whose name are in the Lambs book of life will walk with him for they are worthy and have not defiled themselves and they have washed both themselves and their garment in the blood of the lamb. Hallelujah.

* * * * * * * * * *

Lord Jesus it not by power neither by my might but your Spirit even your grace, I pray you preserve me unto your coming and may I be found worthy to walk with you in white. Amen.

* * * * * * * * * * *

If He had wanted to die as a king he is, he would not have died on the cross being naked publicly and shamefully. But there is no other way man will be saved if not on the cross, he took it upon himself for you and I because he loved us. If Christ can still go on for our sake, even when friends, family and mostly his Father turned back on him for our sins, then what's too much for you to do for him? We have chosen to complain and to be ungrateful instead of giving thanks, we have chosen to be sinful and crucify him the second time instead of to show appreciation for dying for our sins. * * * * * * * "My lord forgive me for even I have crucified you the second time, and by your grace I was delivered and was made to know the consequences of such, and now O Lord, thou hast set me upon the rock that I may live in thy Son to please you in all my ways. I pray more and more grace even as thou have given it abundantly. Amen.

* * * * * * * * * * * *

Now if Christ will spread out his aims, and give out his hands that he be nailed on a tree, on the right hand, they nailed, he shouted and cried out, the same they did to his left hand even as they lay him on the cross, there was no other thing he can see if not the Heaven which he faced, in tears, pains and agony he cried loud to God His Father. The soldiers held him as strong as they nailed him to the cross, "Father! Father!! "Jesus cried aloud to God in tears, all for our sake. They lifted the Son of Man up publicly, showing his nakedness to all, he was not ashamed to die on our behalf on that manner. We mocked him, laughed at him, but at that, he prayed for us saying "Father forgive them for they know not what they are doing". Jesus waited to hear from his Father but there was no communication anymore, then he cried again saying in Matthew 27:46 ".... Eli, Eli, Lama sabachthani? That is to say, My God, My God, why hast thou forsaken me? After which He committed his Spirit into Gods hand and gave up. Jesus descended to hell and came out victoriously and triumphantly, he defeated death and its sting, and later ascended to Heaven after he had shown himself to his disciples. Then, he sent down to us the Holy Spirit as he has promised and gave much of his grace to see what then we can do for him to expand his kingdom, since he has done us good while on earth, even still doing us good now in Heaven, but the question still remains, what have you done for Christ Jesus, seeing that he has done all this for you? Are you confused on what to do for Christ Jesus? Now these are what's required of us

1) Give your life to him by being a born again in him (if you have not).

2) Be baptized of the water (Mansion baptism).

3) receive the Holy Spirit and also be baptized of Him (By fire).

4) Awake to righteousness and forsake sin and evil deeds, and study His Words (Bible) in order to conquer all things.

5) Perfect your faith and salvation in Holiness (Both of inside and outside).

6) Evangelize/preach (both in words and exemplary life) the gospel to every creature 7) As you receive Christ, walk also in him, finally as you live in the Spirit also walk in the Spirit that you may please God and not fulfill the lust of the flesh. Every other things shall you be thought by him (Holy Spirit). May the LORD keep and sustain us all in faith through our Lord Jesus Christ, Amen.

https://www.facebook.com/evangelistmichaelolua

About The Author

Evangelist Michael C. Olua

Evangelist Michael C. Olua is the founder of JESUS for all SOULS, a ministry given to him by the LORD JESUS Christ, for evangelical outreaches and discipleship, both in cities and villages. Evangelist Michael C. Olua has a passion for the Gospel and to see men and women come to JESUS Christ. He is fully trusting God for His promise to be "His light to both the lost and the Church with the preaching of the Gospel of Love, holiness, righteousness, heaven and hell by the Power of the Holy Spirit". He holds weekly Bible study through the social platform in other to reach out to those far. He is married to Chioma, with kids.

www.ingramcontent.com/pod-product-compliance
Lightning Source LLC
LaVergne TN
LVHW020544160826
845677LV00015B/4192
* 9 7 9 8 8 4 4 1 1 3 1 0 9 *